ROCKY Planets

Kyla Steinkraus

Rourke
Educational Media

rourkeeducationalmedia.com

Scan for Related Titles
and Teacher Resources

Teaching Focus:

Concepts of Print: Have students find capital letters and punctuation in a sentence. Ask students to explain the purpose for using them in a sentence.

Before Reading:

Building Academic Vocabulary and Background Knowledge

Before reading a book, it is important to set the stage for your child or student by using pre-reading strategies. This will help them develop their vocabulary, increase their reading comprehension, and make connections across the curriculum.

1. Read the title and look at the cover. *Let's make predictions about what this book will be about.*
2. Take a picture walk by talking about the pictures/photographs in the book. Implant the vocabulary as you take the picture walk. Be sure to talk about the text features such as headings, Table of Contents, glossary, bolded words, captions, charts/diagrams, or Index.
3. Have students read the first page of text with you then have students read the remaining text.
4. Strategy Talk – use to assist students while reading.
   - Get your mouth ready
   - Look at the picture
   - Think…does it make sense
   - Think…does it look right
   - Think…does it sound right
   - Chunk it – by looking for a part you know
5. Read it again.
6. After reading the book complete the activities below.

Content Area Vocabulary
Use glossary words in a sentence.

atmosphere
axis
gravity
orbits
rotates
solar system

After Reading:

Comprehension and Extension Activity

After reading the book, work on the following questions with your child or students in order to check their level of reading comprehension and content mastery.

1. *How many planets are in our solar system?* (Summarize)
2. *What planet do we live on?* (Text to self connection)
3. *Which planets are the rocky planets?* (Summarize)
4. *Why do scientists send rovers to other planets?* (Asking questions)

Extension Activity

Create a poster of the four rocky planets! Draw each planet and provide at least two bullet points that describe each planet. Don't forget to label each planet and create a title for your poster.

Table of Contents

hen you look up
the sky at night,
t do you see?
solar system
ade up of the
ions of objects
e sky above us.
se include the
, Moon, stars,

Sun

A planet is a round body in space that circles, or **orbits**, the Sun. A planet also **rotates**, or spins, on its **axis**.

The Earth's axis is tilted on its orbital plane. This is what causes the seasons.

Every planet moves at a different speed. A year is the amount of time it takes a planet to orbit the Sun once. A day is the amount of time it takes for a planet to rotate once. Years and days are different for each planet.

March 21
beginning of spring

June 21
beginning of summer

December 22
beginning of winter

September 23
beginning of autumn

On Earth, a day is 24 hours. A year is 365 days.

There are eight planets in our solar system. The four planets closest to the Sun are known as the rocky planets. They are Mercury, Venus, Earth, and Mars. They are made mostly of rock with an iron core.

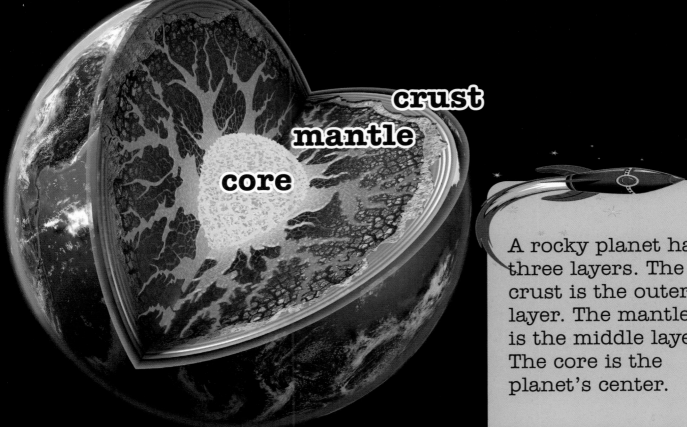

crust

mantle

core

A rocky planet has three layers. The crust is the outer layer. The mantle is the middle layer. The core is the planet's center.

Up Close with Mercury

Mercury is closest to the Sun, so it is extremely hot and dry. Because it has no **atmosphere**, or air, there are no clouds or wind.

Sun

Mercury

Venus

Earth

Mars

Jupiter

Saturn

Mercury is the smallest planet.

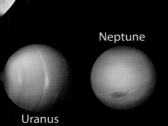

Uranus

Neptune

Mercury has many plains and craters, just like our Moon. It also takes a shorter time to orbit the Sun. An entire year on Mercury lasts only 88 days.

Lovely Venus

Venus is dry, rocky, and covered with volcanoes. Solid lava covers 85 percent of the planet's surface.

Thick, poisonous orange clouds make Venus dark and gloomy. The atmosphere is so heavy, it could crush you in seconds.

Venus is also the hottest planet, much hotter than your oven at home!

The planet Venus has extremely high temperatures that reach almost 900° Fahrenheit (480° Celsius).

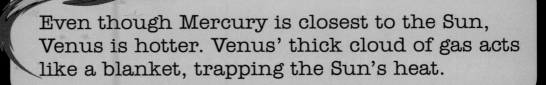

Even though Mercury is closest to the Sun, Venus is hotter. Venus' thick cloud of gas acts like a blanket, trapping the Sun's heat.

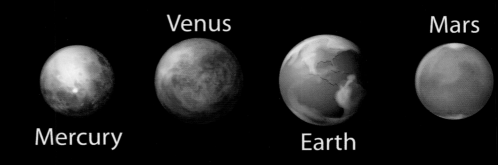

Mercury

Venus

Earth

Mars

It takes longer for Venus to rotate one time than to orbit the Sun. So one day on Venus is longer than a year!

Home, Sweet Home

Earth's distance from the Sun is just right, not too hot or too cold. Earth is the only planet with the right atmosphere and enough water to support life.

Earth is known as the blue planet because it appears blue from space. This is because 70 percent of the Earth's surface is water!

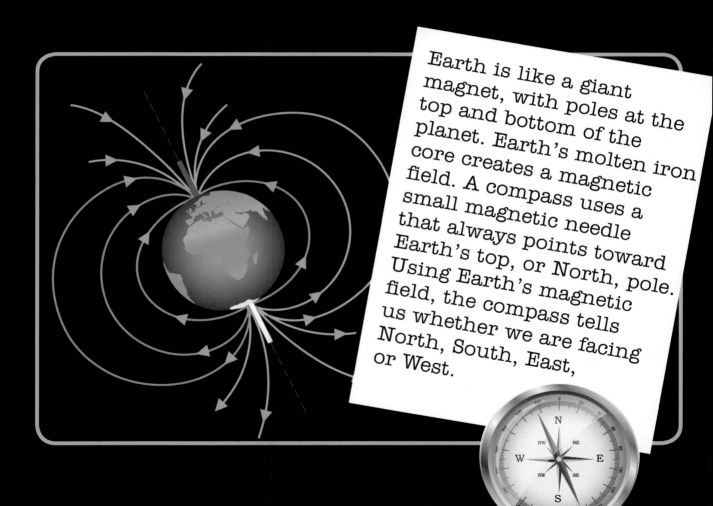

Earth is like a giant magnet, with poles at the top and bottom of the planet. Earth's molten iron core creates a magnetic field. A compass uses a small magnetic needle that always points toward Earth's top, or North, pole. Using Earth's magnetic field, the compass tells us whether we are facing North, South, East, or West.

The Red Planet

While Venus and Mercury are very hot, Mars is extremely cold. It is a freezing desert with wild, whirling dust storms.

Mars is called the red planet because of the rusty red rock and sand covering its surface.

An average day on Mars is colder than the Antarctic!

one-third of Earth's, you could jump three times higher on Mars!

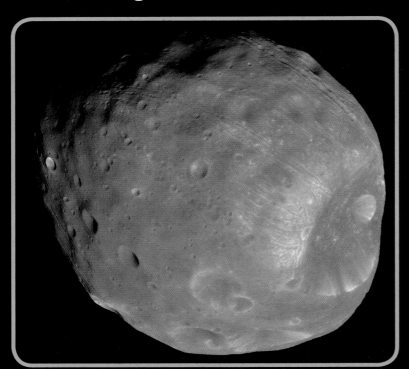

Phobos, the biggest of the Mars' moons

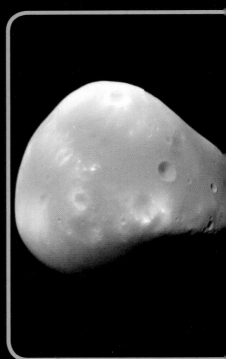

Deimos, the smaller of Mars' moons

Mars has two moons. Earth has one. Mercury and Venus have none.

Scientists have sent four rovers to explore Mars' surface. Remote-controlled from Earth, they spend years collecting data and pictures for scientists to study.

Neighbors in Space

The more we study the rocky planets, the more we are able to learn about our fascinating neighbors in space.

Mars

Earth

Venus

Mercury

Someday, we may even be able to visit the planets. Which one would you visit?

Backyard Astronomy

With a parent to help you, gather the needed supplies. First, tape the red cellophane over the top of the flashlight. The red light will allow you to see the sky chart and compass without impairing your night vision.

Now you can read the sky chart to identify the planets and stars and direct you where to look in the sky. Use the compass to help you face the correct direction. Finally, use your binoculars or telescope to see the planets close up!

★★★

Equipment Needed:

binoculars or telescope

sky chart

compass

flashlight

red cellophane

Index

Websites

www.amazing-space.stsci.edu/
www.nasa.gov/audience/forkids/kidsclub/flash/index.html#.UqSyye
    LOR7x
www.starchild.gsfc.nasa.gov/docs/
    StarChild/StarChild.html

Meet The Author!
www.meetREMauthors.com

About the Author

Kyla Steinkraus lives with her husband and two children in Tampa, Florida. She enjoys drawing, photography, and writing. On hot summer nights, her family likes to lie down in the grass and gaze up at the sky.

PHOTO CREDITS: Cover © tuntekron petsajun; page 4-5 © dalmingo, Earth © Ibooo7; page 6 © LSkywalker, page 7 © XYZ; page 8-9 © BlueRingMedia, page 9,10, 14, 16 © Tristan3D; page 11 © Elenarts; page 12, 17, 18 courtesy of NASA, page 13 © BlueRingMedia; page 15 © Snowbelle, compass © olegganko; page 19 © James Steidl; page 20 © Vadim Sadovski, page 21 © Pete Pahham; page 22 top to bottom © Pete Pahham, Ibooo7, Asier Romero; page 23 top to bottom © dalmingo, LSkywalker, Vadim Sadovski

Edited by: Jill Sherman

Cover design and Interior design: by Nicola Stratford
nicolastratford.com

Library of Congress PCN Data

Rocky Planets / Kyla Steinkraus
(Inside Outer Space)
ISBN 978-1-62717-727-6 (hard cover)
ISBN 978-1-62717-849-5 (soft cover)
ISBN 978-1-62717-961-4 (e-Book)
Library of Congress Control Number: 2014935653

Rourke Educational Media
Printed in the United States of America, North Mankato, Minnesota

Also Available as:
ROURKE'S e-Books